I0410229

Table Of Contents

Chapter 1: Introduction to Podcasting

- Understanding the podcasting landscape
- Benefits and potential of podcasting
- Identifying your niche and target audience

Chapter 2: Preparing Your Podcast Idea

- Brainstorming and refining your podcast concept
- Researching your niche and competition
- Defining your unique selling proposition (USP)

Chapter 3: Planning and Content Creation

- Structuring your podcast episodes
- Creating compelling episode titles and descriptions
- Outlining episode content and scripting
- Developing a content calendar

Chapter 4: Setting Up Your Recording Space

- Choosing the right recording equipment
- Microphones, headphones, and other essential gear
- Acoustic treatment and improving sound quality

Chapter 5: Recording Techniques and Best Practices

- Tips for effective recording sessions
- Microphone etiquette and speaking techniques
- Conducting interviews and engaging conversations

Chapter 6: Editing and Post-Production

- Introduction to podcast editing software
- Editing out mistakes and improving pacing
- Adding music, sound effects, and transitions
- Balancing audio levels for a polished result

Chapter 7: Crafting Captivating Intros and Outros

- Importance of strong podcast intros
- Creating a memorable podcast intro
- Crafting compelling outro messages

Chapter 8: Publishing and Distribution

- Choosing a podcast hosting platform
- Submitting your podcast to directories (Apple Podcasts, Spotify, etc.)
- Understanding RSS feeds and syndication
- Scheduling and releasing episodes

Chapter 9: Building an Engaged Audience

- Effective podcast promotion strategies
- Utilizing social media and online communities
- Collaborating with other podcasters and influencers
- Encouraging listener interaction and feedback

Chapter 10: Monetization and Sponsorships

- Exploring different monetization options (ads, memberships, donations)
- Attracting potential sponsors and advertisers
- Creating value for your sponsors and maintaining authenticity

Chapter 11: Continuous Improvement and Growth

- Importance of analyzing podcast performance
- Using listener feedback to refine your content
- Evolving your podcast format and style over time

Chapter 12: Overcoming Challenges and Staying Motivated

- Dealing with technical difficulties and setbacks
- Managing time and staying consistent
- Finding inspiration and maintaining passion

Chapter 13: Legal and Copyright Considerations

- Understanding copyright and fair use
- Licensing music and other audio materials
- Addressing potential legal issues in podcasting

Chapter 14: Expanding Your Podcasting Empire

- Launching additional podcasts or spin-offs
- Creating supplementary content (blogs, videos, etc.)
- Building a personal brand around your podcasts

Chapter 15: Success Stories and Lessons Learned

- Interviews with successful podcasters
- Analyzing their journeys and strategies
- Extracting key takeaways for your own podcasting journey

Epilogue: Your Podcasting Legacy

- Reflecting on your podcasting experience
- Celebrating milestones and achievements
- Inspiring future podcasters

Appendices:

- Glossary of podcasting terms
- Sample podcast episode outline and script
- Checklist for launching a new podcast

This book will provide aspiring podcasters with a comprehensive roadmap to not only start their podcasting journey but also thrive in the ever-evolving digital audio landscape. Through practical advice, real-world examples, and actionable strategies, readers will gain the knowledge and confidence needed to create and grow successful podcasts that resonate with their target audiences.

Chapter 1: Introduction to Podcasting

In the modern digital age, podcasting has emerged as a powerful medium for communication, education, entertainment, and connection. As a podcast host, you have the unique opportunity to reach a global audience and share your ideas, stories, and expertise in an engaging and accessible format. In this chapter, we'll dive into the fundamentals of podcasting, exploring the landscape, benefits, and the crucial process of identifying your niche and target audience.

Understanding the Podcasting Landscape

Podcasting, in essence, is the creation and distribution of audio content that listeners can stream or download online. Unlike radio broadcasts, podcasts offer the flexibility to listeners, allowing them to choose when and where they consume content. This on-demand nature of podcasting has contributed to its rapid growth and popularity.

Podcasts cover a wide range of topics, from news and interviews to storytelling, education, self-improvement, true crime, pop culture, and beyond. As a result, the podcasting landscape is diverse and ever-expanding, providing opportunities for creators from all walks of life to share their passions and expertise.

Benefits and Potential of Podcasting

In the ever-evolving world of digital media, podcasting has emerged as a dynamic and impactful platform that offers a plethora of benefits and potential for creators, entrepreneurs, and individuals alike. This chapter delves deep into the advantages of podcasting, exploring how this medium has transformed the way we consume content and connect with audiences.

1. Accessibility and Convenience: Podcasting breaks down geographical barriers, enabling creators to reach a global audience. Listeners can consume podcasts anytime, anywhere, whether they're commuting, exercising, or multitasking. This accessibility enhances the overall user experience and makes podcasting a versatile medium.

2. Intimate Connection: The power of the human voice fosters a unique and personal connection between podcast hosts and their listeners. This intimacy allows for deeper engagement, as listeners feel like they're part of a meaningful conversation. The authentic and relatable nature of podcasting builds trust and loyalty over time.

3. Niche Engagement: Podcasting caters to a diverse array of interests and niches. Creators can tailor their content to specific audiences, allowing them to connect with individuals who share their passions. This targeted approach results in a highly engaged and dedicated listener base.

4. Multitasking-Friendly: Podcasts fit seamlessly into listeners' busy lives. People can listen while performing tasks that don't require their full attention, such as driving, exercising, or doing household chores. This multitasking-friendly aspect of podcasts sets them apart from other forms of media.

5. Authenticity and Authority: Podcasting offers a platform for creators to showcase their expertise, share stories, and express their genuine selves. This authenticity helps build credibility and positions hosts as authorities in their respective fields.

6. Storytelling Opportunities: Podcasts are an ideal medium for storytelling. Creators can weave narratives, share personal experiences, and captivate listeners with engaging audio content. Storytelling not only entertains but also fosters emotional connections.

7. Monetization Avenues: Podcasters can explore various monetization strategies, such as sponsorships, advertising, merchandise sales, premium content subscriptions, and crowdfunding. These avenues offer creators opportunities to turn their passion into a sustainable income source.

8. Networking and Collaboration: Podcasting facilitates collaboration and networking within your niche. Interviewing guests, co-hosting episodes, or participating in podcasting communities can lead to valuable connections and partnerships.

9. Building a Personal Brand: Creating a podcast provides a platform to establish and grow your personal brand. Sharing your expertise and insights can elevate your visibility and reputation within your industry.

10. Evergreen Content: Unlike live broadcasts, podcasts are evergreen content. Once published, episodes remain available for new listeners to discover, providing ongoing value and exposure.

11. Empowerment and Expression: Podcasting empowers individuals to have a voice and share their perspectives on a global scale. It's a medium for expressing opinions, sparking discussions, and advocating for change.

12. Low Entry Barrier: Starting a podcast doesn't require extensive technical expertise or costly equipment. Basic recording equipment and editing software are sufficient to produce quality content.

The potential of podcasting is vast and multifaceted. Whether you're an entrepreneur seeking to connect with your target audience, an educator sharing valuable knowledge, or an individual with a compelling story to tell, podcasting offers a platform to amplify your voice and make a meaningful impact. As you embark on your podcasting journey, keep these benefits in mind, and leverage them to create engaging, informative, and entertaining content that resonates with your audience.

Identifying Your Niche and Target Audience

One of the critical factors in podcasting success is defining your niche and understanding your target audience. Your niche is the specific topic or theme around which your podcast revolves. Choosing a niche allows you to differentiate your podcast and attract a dedicated audience.

Consider the following steps when identifying your niche and target audience:

1. **Passion and Knowledge:** Select a niche that aligns with your passions and expertise. Authenticity and genuine interest will resonate with your audience.
2. **Market Research:** Investigate the demand for podcasts within your chosen niche. Analyze existing podcasts to identify gaps or opportunities for differentiation.
3. **Audience Persona:** Create a detailed profile of your ideal listener, including demographics, interests, behaviors, and pain points. This will guide your content creation.
4. **Narrowing Down:** Refine your niche to a specific and focused topic. A niche that's too broad may struggle to capture a dedicated audience.
5. **Value Proposition:** Define what unique value you'll provide to your listeners. Why should they choose your podcast over others?

As you embark on your podcasting journey, remember that your niche and target audience will guide your content, branding, and overall podcast strategy. By understanding the podcasting landscape, recognizing its benefits, and honing in on your niche, you'll set a strong foundation for creating a podcast that resonates with listeners and sets you up for success.

Chapter 2: Preparing Your Podcast Idea

A successful podcast begins with a well-prepared and unique podcast idea. This chapter guides you through the essential steps of brainstorming, refining your podcast concept, researching your niche and competition, and defining your unique selling proposition (USP). By laying a strong foundation, you'll set yourself up for a compelling and engaging podcast that captures your audience's attention.

Brainstorming and Refining Your Podcast Concept:

The heart of a successful podcast lies in its concept. In this chapter, we'll explore the creative process of brainstorming and refining your podcast idea. By delving deep into your interests, finding a unique angle, and fine-tuning your concept, you'll create a foundation for captivating content that resonates with your audience.

Explore Your Passions:

1. **Passion Mapping:** Start by listing your passions, hobbies, and areas of expertise. Consider what genuinely excites you and fuels your curiosity.
2. **Personal Stories:** Reflect on personal experiences, challenges you've overcome, or journeys you've embarked upon. Sharing your story can form the core of your podcast.

Identify Your Angle:

1. **Narrowing Down:** From your list of passions, identify those that can serve as potential podcast topics. Narrow down your options to focus on the most compelling and relevant ones.

2. **Unique Perspective:** Think about your unique perspective or expertise that you can bring to the chosen topic. What sets you apart from other podcasters discussing similar subjects?

Content and Format:

1. **Content Themes:** Outline key themes and topics within your chosen niche. Consider recurring segments, guest interviews, educational content, storytelling, or a combination of these.
2. **Format Exploration:** Explore various podcast formats, such as solo episodes, co-hosted discussions, interviews, narrative storytelling, or a hybrid approach that suits your content.

Refining Your Concept:

1. **Audience Relevance:** Evaluate how well your chosen concept aligns with the interests and needs of your intended audience. Will your content resonate with them?
2. **Solving Problems:** Consider how your podcast can provide solutions, insights, or entertainment that addresses challenges faced by your audience within your chosen niche.
3. **Focus and Clarity:** Refine your concept to ensure it's clear, focused, and well-defined. Avoid being too broad, as a well-defined niche attracts a more dedicated audience.

Test Your Concept:

1. **Feedback Loop:** Share your podcast concept with trusted friends, family, or peers. Gather feedback on its appeal, clarity, and potential for engagement.
2. **Pilot Episode:** Create a pilot episode or teaser to give your audience a taste of what's to come. Gauge their reactions and adjust your concept if needed.

Flexibility and Evolution:

1. **Open to Evolution:** Be open to refining your concept over time based on audience feedback and changing trends. Podcasts can evolve and adapt as they grow.
2. **Iterative Approach:** Think of your initial episodes as prototypes. Embrace a continuous improvement mindset, refining your concept as you learn from each episode.

Researching Your Niche and Competition:

Understanding your podcast's niche and the competitive landscape is crucial for creating content that stands out and resonates with your target audience. In this chapter, we'll delve into the essential steps of researching your niche and competition, enabling you to make informed decisions and carve a unique space within the podcasting world.

Understanding Your Niche:

1. **Niche Definition:** Clearly define the specific subject area your podcast will cover. This could be a hobby, industry, lifestyle, or any topic that you're passionate about.
2. **Keyword Analysis:** Research relevant keywords and phrases associated with your niche. This will help you understand how your target audience searches for content.
3. **Niche Trends:** Stay updated with current trends, developments, and conversations within your chosen niche. This knowledge will inform your content creation strategy.

Identifying Your Competition:

1. **Podcast Directories:** Explore podcast directories like Apple Podcasts, Spotify, and Google Podcasts to find podcasts in your niche. Take note of their titles, descriptions, and episode topics.
2. **Social Media Search:** Use social media platforms to search for hashtags, groups, and pages related to your niche. Engaging in these communities can provide insights into popular discussions.

3. **Google Search:** Conduct Google searches for keywords within your niche. Analyze the top-ranking websites, blogs, and podcasts to understand the existing competition.

Analyzing Your Competition:

1. **Content Review:** Listen to episodes of competing podcasts. Pay attention to their style, tone, format, and the value they provide to their listeners.
2. **Engagement and Audience:** Look for signs of engagement, such as podcast reviews, social media interactions, and comments on blog posts. This indicates audience interest.
3. **Content Gaps:** Identify areas within your niche that are underserved or haven't been covered extensively. These gaps present opportunities for differentiation.

Differentiating Your Podcast:

1. **Unique Angle:** Determine how your podcast can approach the niche from a unique perspective. Your angle should set you apart and offer a fresh take on familiar topics.
2. **Value Proposition:** Define the value your podcast brings to listeners. What makes your content stand out and why should people choose to listen to your podcast?
3. **Content Variety:** Offer a variety of content formats within your niche. For example, if you're discussing health, you could have expert interviews, personal stories, and educational segments.

Incorporating Research into Your Strategy:

1. **Content Calendar:** Use your research insights to create a content calendar. Plan episodes that address specific topics, trends, and gaps identified in your research.
2. **Guest Selection:** Consider inviting guests who can provide unique insights or perspectives within your niche. This adds diversity and credibility to your podcast.

3. **Engagement Strategies:** Leverage your research to engage with your target audience on social media and other platforms. Join conversations, ask questions, and share your expertise.

Researching your niche and competition is a vital step in podcast preparation. By understanding the landscape, identifying your competition, and finding ways to differentiate your podcast, you'll be equipped to create content that appeals to your audience's interests and needs. Use this research as a foundation for your content strategy, allowing you to produce valuable and engaging episodes that resonate with your target listeners.

Defining Your Unique Selling Proposition (USP):

In a sea of podcasts, a strong and distinctive Unique Selling Proposition (USP) is what will set your show apart and attract a loyal audience. In this chapter, we'll delve into the process of defining your podcast's USP, which is the essence of what makes your content unique, valuable, and appealing to your target listeners.

Understanding the Importance of USP:

1. **Differentiation:** Your USP highlights what sets your podcast apart from others in the same niche. It gives listeners a reason to choose your show over competing options.
2. **Audience Attraction:** A well-defined USP resonates with your target audience, drawing them in and creating a sense of connection.
3. **Consistency:** Your USP guides content creation, ensuring that each episode aligns with your podcast's unique identity.

Identifying Your Podcast's Strengths:

1. **Self-Assessment:** Reflect on your strengths as a host and creator. What unique qualities, skills, or experiences do you bring to the table?
2. **Content Focus:** Consider the main themes and topics your podcast will cover. How does your perspective or approach differ from others?

3. **Audience Alignment:** How well does your personal background and expertise align with the interests and needs of your target audience?

Addressing Audience Needs:

1. **Audience Research:** Gather insights into your target audience's preferences, pain points, and desires. What do they seek in a podcast within your niche?
2. **Solution-Oriented:** Your USP can revolve around solving specific challenges or providing answers to questions that your audience is seeking.

Crafting Your USP:

1. **Clear Statement:** Develop a concise statement that encapsulates your podcast's USP. This statement should be easy to understand and resonate with your target audience.
2. **Value Proposition:** Highlight the value that your podcast offers to listeners. Explain how your content enriches their lives, knowledge, or experiences.
3. **Unique Angle:** Identify the unique angle, perspective, or format that makes your podcast stand out. This could involve storytelling, expert insights, diverse guests, or a specific theme.

Testing and Refining Your USP:

1. **Feedback Loop:** Share your USP with trusted individuals and potential listeners. Gather feedback to ensure that your message is clear and compelling.
2. **Adaptation:** Be prepared to refine your USP as you gain more insight into your audience's preferences and as your podcast evolves over time.

Consistency and Authenticity:

1. **Align with Content:** Ensure that your podcast's episodes, branding, and messaging align with your USP. Consistency reinforces your podcast's identity.
2. **Authenticity Matters:** Your USP should reflect your genuine passion and expertise. Authenticity builds trust and connection with your audience.

Defining your podcast's Unique Selling Proposition (USP) is a critical step in standing out in the podcasting landscape. By identifying your strengths, addressing audience needs, and crafting a clear and compelling USP statement, you create a distinct identity for your podcast. Your USP not only attracts listeners but also guides your content creation, ensuring that each episode aligns with your podcast's unique appeal and provides value to your audience.

In Summary:

Preparing your podcast idea is a pivotal step in launching a successful podcast. Through brainstorming, refining your concept, researching your niche and competition, and defining your unique selling proposition, you establish a solid foundation for creating content that resonates with your target audience. The effort invested in shaping your podcast idea will ultimately contribute to the uniqueness and attractiveness of your podcast, setting the stage for a captivating and impactful show.

Chapter 3: Planning and Content Creation

Podcast episodes that are well-structured and thoughtfully organized are more likely to resonate with your audience and keep them engaged. In this chapter, we'll delve into the process of planning and structuring your podcast episodes to ensure a cohesive and engaging listening experience.

1.
   o   Start with a catchy introduction that hooks your audience.
   o   Introduce yourself and provide a brief overview of the episode's topic.
   o   Set the tone and create anticipation for what's to come.
2.
   o   Divide your main content into segments or sections that logically flow.
   o   Explore the topic in depth, providing valuable information, insights, and examples.
   o   Use storytelling, anecdotes, or case studies to illustrate key points.
3.
   o   Use smooth transitions to connect different segments or topics.
   o   Summarize the key points before transitioning to the next part.
   o   Maintain a logical and coherent progression throughout the episode.
4.
   o   Choose a format that aligns with your podcast's style and goals.

- Incorporate elements like interviews, listener questions, or expert insights to add variety.

5.
- Encourage listener engagement by posing questions or suggesting actions.
- Promote interaction through social media, email, or a dedicated website.

1. Determine an appropriate episode length based on your niche and audience preferences. Avoid dragging on or rushing through content.
2. Maintain a steady pace to keep listeners engaged. Avoid prolonged monologues or excessive pauses.

1. Decide whether you'll follow a scripted, semi-scripted, or more conversational style. Choose what feels natural for you while ensuring clarity.
2. Thoroughly research your topic to provide accurate and valuable insights. Cite sources if necessary to enhance credibility.
3. Practice delivering your content to improve fluency and minimize stumbling during recording.

1. If relevant, consider incorporating visual aids like diagrams, images, or slides that complement your audio content.
2. Use relevant audio clips, sound effects, or music to enhance the overall listening experience.

The structure of your podcast episodes greatly influences how well your content is received by your audience. By planning and organizing your episodes thoughtfully, you create a cohesive and engaging listening experience. Remember to choose a format that aligns with your podcast's style, maintain a balanced pace, and encourage interaction with your listeners. With a well-structured approach, you'll create content that informs, entertains, and resonates with your audience.

Crafting attention-grabbing episode titles and descriptions is essential for attracting listeners and providing a clear understanding of your podcast's content. In this chapter, we'll explore the art of creating compelling episode titles and descriptions that entice your audience to tune in and engage with your podcast.

1. Ensure that your title accurately represents the episode's content. Avoid clickbait and misleading titles.
2. Use action verbs, intriguing adjectives, or questions to spark curiosity and encourage clicks.
3. Incorporate relevant keywords that reflect the episode's topic. This improves discoverability in search results.
4. Keep titles concise while conveying the essence of the episode. Aim for around 5-8 words for maximum impact.
5. Highlight a key point, insight, or teaser in the title to pique listeners' curiosity.

1. Summarize the episode's content in a clear and concise manner. Keep descriptions between 1-3 paragraphs.
2. Provide a sneak peek into the episode's highlights, discussions, or key takeaways. Leave listeners wanting more.
3. Highlight the benefits listeners will gain from tuning in. Explain why this episode is worth their time.
4. Infuse your unique podcasting style and voice into the description. Make it relatable and inviting.

5. Encourage listeners to engage further, such as subscribing, sharing, or visiting your website for additional resources.

1. Maintain a consistent style for your episode titles and descriptions that aligns with your podcast's branding.
2. If applicable, include episode numbers in your titles for easy reference and navigation.

1. Research relevant SEO keywords related to your episode's topic. Incorporate these keywords naturally in titles and descriptions.
2. Optimized titles and descriptions improve your podcast's visibility in search results on platforms like Apple Podcasts and Google Podcasts.

1. Periodically test different titles and descriptions for similar episodes to see which ones attract more clicks and engagement.
2. Use podcasting platforms' analytics to track the performance of different titles and descriptions.

Compelling episode titles and descriptions are your podcast's marketing tools to capture the attention of potential listeners. By ensuring clarity, using engaging language, and conveying the episode's value, you'll entice your audience to click and listen. Consistency in branding and SEO optimization further enhance your podcast's discoverability. With careful crafting and experimentation, your episode titles and descriptions will be powerful tools to attract and engage your audience.

Creating well-structured and engaging podcast episodes requires a thoughtful approach to outlining content and scripting. In this chapter, we'll explore the process of outlining your episode content and scripting, ensuring that you deliver valuable and captivating episodes to your listeners.

1. Identify the main points, key ideas, or segments you want to cover in the episode.
2. Organize your points in a logical order to create a coherent and easy-to-follow episode structure.
3. Break down complex ideas into subtopics or segments, making it easier for listeners to digest the content.
4. Incorporate relevant stories, anecdotes, or examples that illustrate your points and engage your audience.
5. If applicable, consider using visual aids or multimedia to complement your audio content.

1. Decide on your preferred scripting style—fully scripted, bullet points, or a more conversational approach.
2. Script a captivating introduction that hooks your audience and introduces the episode's topic.
3. Write out your main talking points, ensuring clarity and coherence. Use concise sentences to keep your content engaging.
4. Script smooth transitions between different segments or subtopics to guide listeners through the episode.
5. Include prompts for audience engagement, such as questions, discussion prompts, or invitations to connect on social media.

1. Rehearse your scripted content to ensure smooth delivery and natural-sounding narration.
2. Make adjustments based on how the content flows during practice. Edit for clarity and coherence.

3. Estimate the time required for each segment to ensure your episode doesn't run too short or too long.

1. Maintain a conversational and authentic tone while reading from your script to keep listeners engaged.
2. Inject emotion, enthusiasm, and appropriate inflection into your voice to convey your passion for the topic.

1. During editing, ensure the content flows smoothly and transitions are seamless.
2. Double-check facts, data, and references to maintain accuracy and credibility.

Outlining episode content and scripting play a pivotal role in creating engaging and informative podcast episodes. By carefully structuring your content, scripting your key points, and practicing your delivery, you'll be well-prepared to produce high-quality episodes that resonate with your audience. Balancing preparation with a natural delivery style ensures that your podcast feels both professional and relatable to your listeners.

A well-structured content calendar is the backbone of a successful podcast. In this chapter, we'll explore the process of developing a content calendar to effectively plan, organize, and create your podcast episodes, ensuring a consistent and engaging experience for your listeners.

1. A content calendar helps you maintain a regular release schedule, keeping your audience engaged and anticipating new episodes.

2. Planning ahead reduces last-minute stress and ensures you have ample time for research, scripting, recording, and editing.
3. A content calendar allows you to mix up episode topics and formats, keeping your content fresh and appealing to a broader audience.

1.
- o Brainstorm a list of themes and topics that align with your podcast's niche and goals.
- o Consider seasonal trends, listener interests, and emerging industry discussions.

2.
- o Determine the importance and relevance of each topic.
- o Prioritize content based on timeliness, audience demand, and potential impact.

3.
- o Decide on your podcast's release frequency (e.g., weekly, bi-weekly, monthly).
- o Choose specific days and times for episode releases to establish a routine for your audience.

4.
- o Define the formats you'll use, such as interviews, solo episodes, case studies, or Q&A sessions.
- o Allocate slots for each format in your content calendar.

5.

Plan special episodes or themed seasons that align with holidays, events, or specific periods of the year.

6.

If you'll be featuring guests, coordinate their availability with your content calendar.

1.

   Create a calendar grid with each month's dates and episode release days.

2.

   o   Assign specific topics or themes to each episode slot on the calendar.
   o   Ensure a balance of diverse topics to keep your content engaging.

3.

   Allocate time for research, outlining, scripting, recording, and editing for each episode.

4.

   Include buffer weeks for unexpected delays or to accommodate emerging trends or breaking news.

5.

   Plan how you'll promote each episode on social media, newsletters, and other platforms.

1.

   Follow your content calendar to ensure consistency and organized content creation.

2.   While sticking to the plan is important, be open to adjusting the calendar based on listener feedback, emerging trends, or unforeseen circumstances.

3.   Periodically review and update your content calendar to ensure it remains relevant and aligned with your podcast's goals.

A content calendar is your roadmap to successful podcasting. By identifying themes, prioritizing content, defining formats, and organizing release schedules, you'll streamline your podcast production process and deliver consistent, valuable, and engaging episodes to your audience. A well-executed content calendar sets the foundation for a podcast that captivates listeners and builds a dedicated following over time.

Chapter 4: Setting Up Your Recording Space

Creating a professional and high-quality podcast requires a well-equipped recording space. In this chapter, we'll guide you through the process of setting up your recording space, including selecting the right recording equipment, choosing microphones and headphones, and implementing acoustic treatment to enhance sound quality.

Choosing the Right Recording Equipment:

1. **Microphone:** Consider options like the **Shure SM7B, Audio-Technica AT2020**, or **Rode Podcaster**. Choose a microphone that suits your voice and recording environment.
2. **Audio Interface:** Opt for interfaces like the **Focusrite Scarlett 2i2** or **PreSonus AudioBox USB** to connect your microphone to your computer.
3. **Headphones:** Invest in closed-back headphones such as the **Audio-Technica ATH-M50x** or **Sony MDR-7506** for accurate monitoring and noise isolation.
4. **Pop Filter:** Attach a **Aokeo Professional Microphone Pop Filter** to reduce plosive sounds during recording.
5. **Boom Arm:** Use a sturdy boom arm like the **Heil Sound PL-2T Overhead Broadcast Boom** to position your microphone comfortably.
6. **Shock Mount:** Mount your microphone on a shock mount like the **Heil Sound PRSM-B Shock Mount** to minimize vibrations and handling noise.

Microphones, Headphones, and Other Essential Gear:

1. **Microphones:** Consider dynamic microphones like the **Shure SM7B**, condenser microphones like the **AKG C214**, or USB microphones like the **Blue Yeti** for ease of use.

2. **Headphones:** Choose over-ear headphones with a flat frequency response to accurately monitor your recordings.
3. **Pop Filter:** A pop filter reduces harsh plosive sounds (like "p" and "b" sounds) that can distort your recording.
4. **Boom Arm:** A boom arm allows you to position your microphone at the optimal distance while maintaining comfort.
5. **Shock Mount:** A shock mount isolates the microphone from vibrations, resulting in cleaner audio.

Acoustic Treatment and Improving Sound Quality:

1. **Acoustic Panels:** Use acoustic panels like the **Auralex Acoustics Studiofoam Panels** to absorb reflections and improve room acoustics.
2. **Bass Traps:** If you have low-frequency issues, consider adding bass traps to control room resonance.
3. **Reflection Filters:** Place reflection filters like the **SE Electronics Reflexion Filter X** around your microphone to reduce reflections.
4. **Desk Pads:** Use desk pads or foam platforms to isolate your microphone from vibrations caused by the desk.
5. **Rearrange Furniture:** Adjust the layout of your room to minimize sound reflections and create an optimal recording environment.

Testing and Calibration:

1. **Recording Tests:** Conduct test recordings to assess audio quality, identify any issues, and make necessary adjustments.
2. **Room Calibration:** Use software like **Room EQ Wizard** to analyze and calibrate your room's acoustics for better sound quality.

In Summary:

Setting up your recording space with the right equipment and acoustic treatment is crucial for producing professional-quality podcast episodes. Choose suitable microphones, headphones, and accessories, and consider acoustic treatment solutions to optimize your recording environment. With careful equipment selection and setup, you'll ensure that your podcast audio is clear, crisp, and engaging for your listeners.

Chapter 5: Recording Techniques and Best Practices

Recording high-quality podcast episodes requires mastering effective recording techniques and adhering to best practices. In this chapter, we'll delve into valuable tips for conducting successful recording sessions, maintaining proper microphone etiquette, refining speaking techniques, and conducting engaging interviews and conversations.

Tips for Effective Recording Sessions:

1. **Preparation:** Set up your recording space, equipment, and materials well in advance to minimize disruptions during recording.
2. **Script Familiarity:** Be well-acquainted with your script or talking points to ensure a smooth delivery and minimize mistakes.
3. **Quiet Environment:** Choose a time for recording when your environment is quiet, and external noises are minimal.
4. **Focus and Energy:** Approach each recording session with enthusiasm and energy to maintain a dynamic and engaging tone.

Microphone Etiquette and Speaking Techniques:

1. **Proximity:** Maintain a consistent distance from your microphone to ensure consistent audio levels and avoid distortion.
2. **Plosives and Sibilance:** Position your microphone at an angle to minimize plosive and sibilant sounds, and maintain proper microphone technique.
3. **Breath Control:** Practice breath control to avoid heavy breathing or distracting pauses during your recording.
4. **Articulation:** Speak clearly and enunciate words to enhance listener comprehension, especially when discussing complex topics.

Conducting Interviews and Engaging Conversations:

1. **Research:** Prepare thorough research on your interviewees or conversation topics to facilitate engaging discussions.
2. **Listening Skills:** Be an active listener during interviews, allowing for natural back-and-forth conversations.
3. **Follow-Up Questions:** Ask follow-up questions to delve deeper into interesting points and encourage insightful responses.
4. **Stay On Track:** While spontaneous moments are valuable, ensure that conversations stay relevant to the episode's theme.

Managing Interviewee Nerves:

1. **Preparation:** Communicate the interview flow and questions in advance to help interviewees feel more comfortable.
2. **Friendly Environment:** Create a friendly and supportive atmosphere to put interviewees at ease.
3. **Encouragement:** Offer positive feedback and encouragement to build interviewee confidence and foster a natural conversation.

Recording and Editing Considerations:

1. **Multiple Takes:** Don't hesitate to re-record segments if necessary to achieve the best possible quality.
2. **Editing:** Edit out any mistakes, pauses, or background noise to maintain a polished final episode.
3. **Natural Editing:** Maintain natural speech patterns and avoid overly heavy editing that can make the conversation sound unnatural.

Mastering recording techniques and best practices enhances the quality of your podcast episodes. Effective recording sessions, microphone etiquette, engaging conversations, and skillful interview techniques contribute to a captivating and professional podcast. By adhering to these principles, you'll create content that resonates with your audience and leaves a lasting impact.

Chapter 6: Editing and Post-Production

The editing and post-production phase is where your raw recordings transform into polished and engaging podcast episodes. In this chapter, we'll introduce you to podcast editing software, guide you through the process of editing out mistakes, enhancing pacing, incorporating music and sound effects, and balancing audio levels for a professional and polished final result.

Introduction to Podcast Editing Software:

1. **Audacity:** A free, open-source audio editing software with essential editing tools and effects.
2. **Adobe Audition:** A professional audio editing software with advanced features and effects.
3. **GarageBand:** Apple's user-friendly software for Mac users, suitable for basic to intermediate editing.
4. **Hindenburg Journalist:** Designed specifically for podcasters, with intuitive features for easy editing.

Editing Out Mistakes and Improving Pacing:

1. **Cutting and Deleting:** Trim unwanted sections, mistakes, pauses, and filler words for smoother pacing.
2. **Breath Removal:** Edit out excessive breath sounds to maintain a professional sound.
3. **Tightening:** Ensure conversations flow naturally by editing out tangents or repetitive segments.

Adding Music, Sound Effects, and Transitions:

1. **Music Selection:** Choose background music that complements your podcast's tone and enhances the listening experience.
2. **Sound Effects:** Incorporate sound effects to emphasize moments, transitions, or add a creative touch.

3. **Transitions:** Use smooth transitions like fades, crossfades, or swells to guide listeners between segments.

Balancing Audio Levels for a Polished Result:

1. **Volume Leveling:** Adjust audio levels to maintain consistent loudness throughout the episode.
2. **Compression:** Apply compression to balance quieter and louder parts, enhancing overall audio quality.
3. **EQ (Equalization):** Fine-tune frequencies to enhance clarity, remove muddiness, and improve audio presence.
4. **De-Essing:** Reduce sibilance (sharp "s" sounds) using de-essing tools for smoother audio.

Noise Reduction and Cleanup:

1. **Noise Reduction:** Use noise reduction tools to eliminate background noise, hums, or hisses.
2. **De-Click and De-Crackle:** Remove clicks, pops, and crackles caused by equipment or recording conditions.
3. **Silence Trimming:** Remove excess silence and gaps to maintain pacing and improve episode flow.

Adding Show Notes and Metadata:

1. **Show Notes:** Write detailed show notes summarizing the episode's content, key points, and any relevant links.
2. **Metadata:** Add episode titles, descriptions, and tags to enhance searchability on podcast platforms.

Quality Control and Exporting:

1. **Review:** Listen to the entire edited episode to ensure smooth transitions, balanced audio, and a polished result.
2. **Exporting:** Export the final episode in the appropriate audio format (MP3, WAV) for podcast distribution.

Editing and post-production elevate your podcast episodes to a professional level. With the right podcast editing software, you can remove mistakes, enhance pacing, add music and sound effects, and balance audio levels for a polished final result. By paying attention to detail and using various editing techniques, you'll create episodes that captivate your audience and leave a lasting impression.

Chapter 7: Crafting Captivating Intros and Outros

The introduction and conclusion of your podcast episodes are key moments that leave a lasting impression on your listeners. In this chapter, we'll explore the importance of strong podcast intros, guide you through creating a memorable podcast intro, and offer insights into crafting compelling outro messages that leave your audience engaged and wanting more.

Importance of Strong Podcast Intros:

1. **First Impressions:** A well-crafted intro sets the tone and captures listeners' attention from the very beginning.
2. **Branding:** Intros reinforce your podcast's identity, making your show recognizable and memorable.
3. **Hooking Interest:** A captivating intro entices listeners to stay tuned for the rest of the episode.

Creating a Memorable Podcast Intro:

1. **Hook:** Start with a hook that piques curiosity or addresses a common pain point of your target audience.
2. **Show Identity:** Introduce your podcast by stating its name, your role, and a brief description of what listeners can expect.
3. **Episode Preview:** Offer a glimpse into the episode's content, highlighting key topics or guests.
4. **Music or Sound Effects:** Incorporate music or sound effects that align with your podcast's theme and create an engaging atmosphere.

Crafting Compelling Outro Messages:

1. **Summarize Key Points:** Recap the main takeaways or highlights from the episode to reinforce its value.
2. **Call to Action (CTA):** Encourage listeners to take action, such as subscribing, leaving a review, or visiting your website.

3. **Teaser for Next Episode:** Give a sneak peek of what's coming in the next episode to keep your audience excited.
4. **Gratitude:** Express gratitude for your listeners' time and engagement, making them feel appreciated.

Consistency and Branding:

1. **Consistent Style:** Maintain a consistent tone, style, and duration for your intros and outros to build familiarity.
2. **Branding Elements:** Incorporate your podcast's logo, tagline, or any signature elements that enhance your brand identity.

Scripting and Delivery:

1. **Scripting:** Write concise and compelling scripts for your intros and outros to ensure clarity and impact.
2. **Delivery:** Deliver intros and outros with enthusiasm, energy, and a genuine connection to your audience.

Editing and Sound Quality:

1. **Audio Quality:** Ensure that intros and outros have the same audio quality as the rest of your episode.
2. **Smooth Transitions:** Use seamless transitions between the main content and intros/outros for a polished listening experience.

Feedback and Refinement:

1. **Listener Feedback:** Pay attention to listener feedback on your intros and outros to make adjustments if necessary.
2. **Evolution:** As your podcast evolves, consider updating your intros and outros to reflect any changes or improvements.

Crafting captivating intros and outros is an essential aspect of podcasting that creates a strong first impression and leaves a memorable last impression on your audience. By understanding the importance of these segments, creating compelling content, and maintaining consistency in branding and delivery, you'll create intros and outros that enhance your podcast's overall quality and listener engagement.

Chapter 8: Publishing and Distribution

Publishing and distributing your podcast effectively is the final step in bringing your episodes to your audience. In this chapter, we'll explore key aspects of this process, including choosing a podcast hosting platform, ensuring proper distribution, and optimizing your podcast for maximum reach.

Choosing a Podcast Hosting Platform:

1. **Libsyn:** A popular and user-friendly hosting platform offering various plans and analytics.
2. **Podbean:** Offers hosting, distribution, monetization options, and customizable podcast websites.
3. **Buzzsprout:** Known for its ease of use, it offers hosting, distribution, and detailed statistics.
4. **Anchor:** A free hosting platform by Spotify, offering easy distribution to various podcast platforms.
5. **Transistor:** Offers hosting, analytics, and team collaboration features.
6. **Blubrry:** Focuses on podcasting with integrated WordPress solutions.
7. **Simplecast:** Offers advanced analytics, distribution, and podcast website features.

Factors to Consider When Choosing a Platform:

1. **Pricing:** Compare pricing plans and features that suit your podcast's needs and budget.
2. **Storage and Bandwidth:** Ensure the platform provides sufficient storage for your episodes and reliable bandwidth.
3. **Distribution:** Confirm that the platform supports distribution to major podcast directories like Apple Podcasts, Spotify, Google Podcasts, and more.
4. **Analytics:** Look for platforms that offer detailed listener analytics to track your podcast's performance.

5. **Monetization:** If you plan to monetize, explore platforms that offer sponsorship or advertising options.
6. **Ease of Use:** Choose a platform that aligns with your technical skills and provides user-friendly tools.

Uploading and Distributing Episodes:

1. **Uploading:** Upload your finalized podcast episodes to your chosen hosting platform.
2. **RSS Feed:** Your platform generates an RSS feed, a crucial link that podcast directories use to syndicate your episodes.
3. **Directory Submission:** Submit your podcast to major directories like Apple Podcasts, Spotify, Google Podcasts, and others using your RSS feed.

Optimizing for Maximum Reach:

1. **Episode Titles and Descriptions:** Craft clear, compelling titles and descriptions that grab attention and accurately represent your episodes.
2. **SEO Optimization:** Use relevant keywords in titles, descriptions, and episode content to improve search visibility.
3. **Cover Art:** Design professional and eye-catching cover art that represents your podcast's theme and attracts potential listeners.
4. **Promotion:** Share episodes on social media, your website, email newsletters, and relevant online communities to expand your podcast's reach.
5. **Consistency:** Maintain a consistent release schedule to keep your audience engaged and attract new listeners.

Choosing a podcast hosting platform is a critical step in ensuring your episodes are distributed to a wide audience. Consider factors like pricing, features, and ease of use when making your decision. Once you've selected a platform, upload your episodes, distribute them to major podcast directories, and optimize your podcast's metadata and promotion strategies to maximize your reach and connect with your target audience effectively.

Submitting Your Podcast to Directories

Getting your podcast listed on popular podcast directories such as Apple Podcasts, Spotify, and Google Podcasts is essential for reaching a wider audience. In this chapter, we'll guide you through the process of submitting your podcast to these directories and ensuring your podcast is discoverable to potential listeners.

Submitting to Apple Podcasts:

1. **Create an Apple ID:** If you don't have one, create an Apple ID or use your existing one.
2. **Podcast Connect:** Go to Apple Podcasts Connect and sign in with your Apple ID.
3. **Add a New Show:** Click the '+' icon to add a new podcast show.
4. **Enter Show Details:** Fill in your podcast's title, description, author, category, and cover art.
5. **Submit Your RSS Feed:** Provide your podcast's RSS feed URL from your hosting platform.
6. **Review and Submit:** Review your details and click "Submit." Apple Podcasts will review your submission before listing your podcast.

Submitting to Spotify:

1. **Spotify for Podcasters:** Visit Spotify for Podcasters and sign in or create an account.
2. **Claim or Add a Podcast:** If your podcast is already on Spotify, claim it using your RSS feed. If not, click "Add a Podcast."
3. **Podcast Details:** Fill in your podcast's details, including title, description, language, and cover art.
4. **RSS Feed Submission:** Provide your podcast's RSS feed URL from your hosting platform.
5. **Verification:** Spotify will verify your ownership of the podcast by sending an email to your podcast's official email address.

6. **Confirmation:** Once verified, your podcast will be added to Spotify's podcast directory.

Submitting to Google Podcasts:

1. **Google Podcasts Manager:** Go to Google Podcasts Manager and sign in or create an account.
2. **Add a Podcast:** Click "Add a Podcast" and provide your podcast's RSS feed URL.
3. **Review Details:** Check your podcast details, including title, author, description, and cover art.
4. **Verification:** Google will send an email to your podcast's official email address for verification.
5. **Confirmation:** After verification, your podcast will be listed on Google Podcasts.

Verification and Review:

1. **Email Verification:** Check your podcast's official email address for verification emails from each directory.
2. **Review Period:** Directory platforms may take some time to review and approve your podcast. Be patient during this process.

Promotion and Optimizing for Discovery:

1. **Share Links:** Once listed, share your podcast's links on your website, social media, and other promotional channels.
2. **Optimize Metadata:** Use relevant keywords, compelling titles, and descriptions to enhance your podcast's discoverability.

Submitting your podcast to directories like Apple Podcasts, Spotify, and Google Podcasts expands your reach and allows potential listeners to find and enjoy your content. Follow the submission processes for each platform, ensure email verification, and optimize your podcast's metadata for maximum discoverability. As your podcast gets listed on major directories, you'll increase your chances of connecting with a wider audience and growing your listener base.

Understanding RSS Feeds and Syndication

RSS feeds and syndication are fundamental concepts in the world of podcasting that enable your episodes to be distributed and easily accessible across various platforms. In this chapter, we'll explore the basics of RSS feeds, how they work, and the concept of syndication that powers the distribution of your podcast episodes.

What is an RSS Feed?

1. **Definition:** RSS stands for "Really Simple Syndication." It's a standardized format for publishing and distributing frequently updated content, like podcast episodes.
2. **Role in Podcasting:** An RSS feed serves as a dynamic link that contains information about your podcast episodes, such as titles, descriptions, audio files, and metadata.
3. **Automatic Updates:** When you publish a new podcast episode, your RSS feed is automatically updated with the episode's details.
4. **Distribution:** Podcast directories and platforms use your podcast's RSS feed to fetch and display your episodes to listeners.

Syndication and Podcast Distribution:

1. **Syndication Process:** Syndication involves sharing your podcast episodes with multiple platforms to reach a broader audience.
2. **Podcast Directories:** Platforms like Apple Podcasts, Spotify, Google Podcasts, and others use your RSS feed to syndicate your episodes to their listeners.
3. **Subscription:** Listeners subscribe to your podcast through their chosen platform, and the platform regularly checks your RSS feed for new episodes.
4. **Episode Updates:** When you release a new episode or update your RSS feed, subscribed platforms automatically fetch and display the new content.

How Syndication Works:

1. **Podcast Hosting Platform:** Your podcast hosting platform generates your podcast's RSS feed.
2. **RSS Feed Contents:** The RSS feed includes details about each episode, such as title, description, audio file URL, and publication date.
3. **Podcast Directories:** Directory platforms use the RSS feed's URL to fetch and display your episodes in their directories.
4. **Subscriptions:** Listeners subscribe to your podcast on directory platforms using your podcast's RSS feed.
5. **Regular Checks:** Directory platforms regularly check the RSS feed for updates and new episodes.

Benefits of RSS Feeds and Syndication:

1. **Wide Reach:** Syndication ensures your episodes are available on various platforms, making them accessible to a larger audience.
2. **Automatic Updates:** New episodes are automatically delivered to subscribers without manual intervention.
3. **Centralized Control:** You manage your podcast's content in one place (your hosting platform), and changes are reflected across all syndicated platforms.

Scheduling and Releasing Episodes

Consistency in episode release is a key factor in building and retaining your podcast audience. In this chapter, we'll explore the importance of scheduling and releasing episodes on a regular basis, as well as strategies for maintaining a consistent podcasting schedule.

Importance of Scheduling and Consistency:

1. **Audience Expectations:** Consistent release schedules build anticipation and trust among your listeners.
2. **Establishing Routine:** Regular episodes help listeners incorporate your podcast into their routine.

3. **Search Rankings:** Consistency can improve your podcast's visibility and rankings on podcast platforms.

Creating a Release Schedule:

1. **Frequency:** Decide how often you'll release new episodes (e.g., weekly, bi-weekly, monthly).
2. **Day and Time:** Choose specific days and times for episode releases to establish a routine for your audience.

Planning and Preparing Episodes:

1. **Content Calendar:** Plan episodes in advance using a content calendar to maintain a steady stream of content.
2. **Batch Recording:** Record multiple episodes in a single session to have a buffer of content ready for release.
3. **Editing and Post-Production:** Allow ample time for editing, adding music/effects, and quality checks.

Announcing Release Dates:

1. **Social Media Teasers:** Tease upcoming episodes on your social media platforms to build excitement.
2. **Newsletter Subscribers:** Notify your email subscribers about upcoming episodes through newsletters.
3. **Website and Blog:** Announce upcoming episodes on your podcast's website or blog.

Releasing Episodes:

1. **Episode Titles and Descriptions:** Craft compelling titles and descriptions that accurately represent the episode's content.
2. **Episode Metadata:** Ensure proper tagging, categorization, and episode numbering.
3. **Promotional Materials:** Prepare accompanying promotional images or graphics for each episode.

Optimizing for Different Time Zones:

1. **Global Audience:** Consider your listeners' time zones when choosing release times.
2. **Multiple Release Times:** Release episodes at different times to cater to various geographic locations.

Dealing with Delays:

1. **Communication:** If you anticipate a delay, inform your audience through social media or an episode update.
2. **Maintaining Transparency:** Address delays honestly and provide an updated release date.

Monitoring Engagement and Feedback:

1. **Listener Feedback:** Pay attention to listener responses and adjust your release schedule based on their preferences.
2. **Analytics:** Use podcast analytics to understand listener behavior and episode performance.

In Summary:

Scheduling and releasing episodes consistently is a cornerstone of successful podcasting. A well-planned release schedule, combined with effective promotion and engagement strategies, helps you build a loyal audience and maintain their interest over time. By understanding the importance of consistency, preparing episodes in advance, and engaging with your listeners, you'll create a podcast that resonates and grows in popularity.

Chapter 9: Building an Engaged Audience

One of the most rewarding aspects of podcasting is connecting with a passionate and engaged audience. In this chapter, we'll explore strategies to effectively promote your podcast, leverage the power of social media and online communities, collaborate with fellow podcasters and influencers, and foster meaningful interaction and feedback from your listeners.

Effective Podcast Promotion Strategies:

Promoting your podcast is essential to reach a wider audience and build a dedicated listener base. Here are some effective strategies to promote your podcast and attract new listeners:

1. **Social Media Promotion:**
   - Share engaging visuals, audiograms, and teaser clips on platforms like Twitter, Instagram, Facebook, and LinkedIn.
   - Utilize relevant hashtags to increase the discoverability of your posts.
   - Run contests, giveaways, or challenges that encourage user participation and sharing.
2. **Cross-Promotion:**
   - Collaborate with other podcasters to feature each other's shows on your episodes.
   - Guest appearances on other podcasts can introduce your content to new audiences.
3. **Email Marketing:**
   - Send regular newsletters to your subscribers to inform them about new episodes and updates.
   - Provide exclusive content or early access to incentivize subscriptions.
4. **Press Releases:**

- Write and distribute press releases for special episodes, milestones, or noteworthy content.
- Reach out to relevant media outlets or bloggers to feature your podcast.

5. **Utilize Your Website and Blog:**
   - Create dedicated podcast pages on your website with episode summaries, player embeds, and links.
   - Write blog posts related to your podcast's topics to attract organic search traffic.

6. **Leverage Podcast Directories:**
   Optimize your podcast's listing on directories like Apple Podcasts, Spotify, and Google Podcasts with compelling descriptions and cover art.

1. **Networking and Events:**
   - Attend industry events, conferences, or meetups to connect with potential listeners and fellow podcasters.
   - Hand out promotional materials like business cards or stickers to spread the word.

2. **Promote on Your Existing Channels:**
   If you have a blog, YouTube channel, or social media following, promote your podcast to your existing audience.

3. **Paid Advertising:**
   Invest in paid social media ads, Google Ads, or podcast promotion platforms to target specific demographics.

4. **SEO Optimization:**
   Use relevant keywords in your podcast's titles, descriptions, and blog posts to improve search visibility.

5. **Engage with Guest Audiences:**
   If you have guest speakers on your podcast, encourage them to promote the episode to their followers.

6. **Launch and Promotion Events:**
   - Host a launch event or live-stream to create buzz around your podcast's debut.
   - Organize special episodes, interviews, or collaborations for promotion events.

Utilizing Social Media and Online Communities:

Social media and online communities are powerful tools for promoting your podcast, connecting with your audience, and building a loyal following. Here are strategies to effectively leverage these platforms:

1. **Choose the Right Platforms:**
   Identify the social media platforms and online communities where your target audience is most active.

2. **Create Engaging Content:**
   - Share teaser clips, quotes, behind-the-scenes glimpses, and visual content related to your episodes.
   - Use eye-catching graphics and images to capture attention and encourage sharing.

3. **Consistent Posting Schedule:**
   Maintain a regular posting schedule to keep your audience engaged and informed.

4. **Interact and Engage:**
   - Respond to comments, questions, and messages promptly to foster genuine interactions.
   - Ask open-ended questions to encourage discussions and engagement.

5. **Use Hashtags Wisely:**
   - Use relevant and trending hashtags to increase the discoverability of your posts.
   - Research popular hashtags in your niche and incorporate them in your content.

6. **Live Streams and Q&A Sessions:**
   Host live sessions to directly engage with your audience, answer their questions, and discuss topics.

7. **Share User-Generated Content:**
   o   Encourage listeners to share their thoughts, fan art, or experiences related to your podcast.
   o   Feature user-generated content on your social media accounts.

1. **Run Contests and Giveaways:**
   o   Organize contests or giveaways that require participants to engage with your content or share your podcast.
   o   Offer podcast-related merchandise or exclusive content as prizes.

1. **Collaborate with Influencers:**
   o   Partner with influencers in your niche to promote your podcast to their followers.
   o   Arrange influencer takeovers or joint content creation for cross-promotion.

2. **Utilize Stories and Polls:**
   o   Use story features on platforms like Instagram and Facebook to share short, engaging content.
   o   Create polls and surveys to involve your audience and gather insights.

3. **Share Listener Feedback:**
   Highlight positive reviews, comments, and feedback from listeners to build social proof.

4. **Promote Special Episodes or Events:**
   Use social media to promote special episodes, live events, or collaborations with enthusiasm.

5. **Create a Community:**

Establish a Facebook Group, subreddit, or other online community where listeners can connect with each other and discuss topics from your podcast.

Tailor your content and engagement strategies to suit each platform's characteristics and the preferences of your target audience. By building an active and engaged online presence, you'll strengthen your podcast's reach and connection with your listeners.

Collaborating with Other Podcasters and Influencers:

Collaborations with fellow podcasters and influencers can expose your podcast to new audiences and create valuable cross-promotional opportunities. Here's how to effectively collaborate and tap into their reach:

1. **Identify Compatible Partners:**
    o   Look for podcasters and influencers whose content aligns with your podcast's niche and values.
    o   Choose collaborators who have an engaged audience that could benefit from your content.
2. **Reach Out with a Clear Proposal:**
    o   Craft a personalized pitch explaining the collaboration idea, its benefits, and how it aligns with their audience's interests.
    o   Highlight how the collaboration will be mutually beneficial.
3. **Joint Episodes:**
    o   Plan joint podcast episodes where both parties contribute insights, stories, or expertise.
    o   Promote the episode on both podcasts and social media to cross-promote to each other's audiences.
4. **Interview Exchanges:**
    o   Invite fellow podcasters or influencers for guest interviews on your podcast, and vice versa.
    o   Share your respective audiences and build credibility through cross-promotion.
5. **Co-Hosted Livestreams or Events:**

- Host live discussions, Q&A sessions, or special events together to engage both audiences in real time.
- Utilize platforms like Instagram Live, Facebook Live, or YouTube Live.

6. **Influencer Shoutouts:**
   - Request influencers to share snippets of your podcast on their social media platforms.
   - Use their endorsement to reach a broader audience.

7. **Guest Blog Posts or Articles:**
   - Collaborate on written content that can be featured on each other's websites or blogs.
   - Share insights, stories, or valuable information related to your podcast.

1. **Content Swaps:**
   - Share short video or audio clips from each other's content on social media platforms.
   - Include a call-to-action to listen to the full episodes on your respective podcasts.

2. **Offer Value to Their Audience:**
   Ensure that the collaboration adds value to their audience's interests, creating a win-win situation.

3. **Follow Up and Maintain Relationships:**
   - Keep the lines of communication open for potential future collaborations.
   - Show appreciation for their involvement and efforts.

4. **Measure Results:**
   Track the impact of collaborations through podcast analytics, social media engagement, and website traffic.

5. **Express Gratitude:**
   Thank your collaborators and promote their content as a gesture of goodwill.

Collaborating with podcasters and influencers can introduce your podcast to new listeners, strengthen your credibility, and broaden your reach within your target niche. Approach collaborations with enthusiasm, professionalism, and a genuine interest in creating valuable content for both your audience and your collaborator's audience.

Encouraging Listener Interaction and Feedback:

1. **Listener Questions:** Dedicate episodes to answering listener questions, fostering a sense of community involvement.
2. **Listener Submissions:** Invite listeners to share personal stories, opinions, or experiences related to your podcast's themes.
3. **Reviews and Ratings:** Encourage listeners to leave reviews and ratings on podcast directories to enhance visibility.

Creating Engaging Content:

1. **Interactive Episodes:** Host live Q&A sessions or interactive discussions to directly engage with listeners.
2. **Contests and Giveaways:** Organize contests or giveaways to reward loyal listeners and attract new ones.

Monitoring Analytics and Engagement:

1. **Podcast Analytics:** Track metrics like downloads, listener locations, and episode popularity to refine your content strategy.
2. **Social Media Insights:** Analyze engagement metrics on social platforms to gauge the effectiveness of your promotional efforts.

In Summary:

Building an engaged audience requires a combination of effective promotion, genuine engagement, collaboration, and a commitment to listener interaction. By implementing these strategies, you'll create a loyal and enthusiastic community around your podcast, fostering a sense of connection and excitement that will contribute to your podcast's growth and success.

Chapter 10: Monetization and Sponsorships

Monetizing your podcast is a rewarding endeavor that can help you generate income from your content creation efforts. In this chapter, we'll delve into various monetization options available to podcasters, including advertising, memberships, and donations.

Exploring Different Monetization Options:

1. **Advertising and Sponsorships:**
   o   Partner with brands or companies to feature sponsored content or ads within your episodes.
   o   Choose sponsors whose products or services align with your podcast's niche and audience.
2. **Dynamic Ad Insertion:**
   Utilize technology to insert targeted ads into your episodes, maximizing relevance and potential earnings.

3. **Affiliate Marketing:**
   Promote affiliate products or services to your listeners and earn a commission for every sale generated through your unique link.

4. **Premium Content or Membership Models:**
   o   Offer exclusive bonus episodes, early access, or ad-free content to subscribers who pay a monthly fee.
   o   Create a membership community with additional perks, like Q&A sessions or merchandise.
5. **Crowdfunding and Donations:**
   Platforms like Patreon allow listeners to support your podcast through monthly donations in exchange for rewards.

6. **Merchandising:**

Design and sell branded merchandise related to your podcast, such as T-shirts, mugs, or stickers.

7. **Live Events and Workshops:**
   Host live events, workshops, or webinars for your audience, charging a fee for participation.

8. **Selling Digital Products:**
   Develop and sell e-books, guides, or online courses related to your podcast's niche.

Preparing for Monetization:

1. **Audience Engagement:** Build a strong and engaged audience before implementing monetization strategies.
2. **Maintain Authenticity:** Choose monetization methods that align with your podcast's content and values to maintain listener trust.
3. **Value Proposition:** Clearly communicate the benefits of supporting your podcast financially to your audience.

Negotiating Sponsorships:

1. **Target Relevant Sponsors:** Approach sponsors whose products or services resonate with your audience.
2. **Professional Proposals:** Create well-structured sponsorship proposals highlighting your podcast's statistics, demographics, and benefits for the sponsor.
3. **Customized Partnerships:** Tailor sponsorship packages to fit the sponsor's goals and audience preferences.
4. **Transparency:** Clearly disclose sponsored content to your audience to maintain transparency and trust.

Managing Monetization Ethically:

1. **Listener Experience:** Prioritize your listeners' experience by maintaining a balance between monetization and content quality.
2. **Avoid Overloading Ads:** Limit the number of ads per episode to prevent listener fatigue.
3. **Value for Supporters:** Ensure that paying subscribers or donors receive meaningful benefits in return.

Legal and Tax Considerations:

1. **Consult Professionals:** Seek legal and tax advice when implementing monetization strategies to ensure compliance.
2. **Disclosure:** Clearly disclose affiliate relationships, sponsored content, and potential conflicts of interest.

Monetizing your podcast requires careful consideration of your audience's preferences, ethical practices, and legal requirements. By offering valuable content and exploring various monetization avenues, you can generate income while maintaining a positive listener experience.

Attracting Potential Sponsors and Advertisers

Attracting sponsors and advertisers to your podcast involves showcasing the value your podcast offers and establishing mutually beneficial partnerships. In this chapter, we'll explore strategies to effectively attract potential sponsors and advertisers to support your podcast.

Understanding Your Podcast's Value:

1. **Audience Insights:** Gather detailed demographic and engagement data about your listeners to present to potential sponsors.
2. **Niche Expertise:** Highlight your expertise in your podcast's niche and how it aligns with the sponsor's target audience.
3. **Content Quality:** Showcase the quality, engagement, and uniqueness of your podcast's content.

Creating a Sponsorship Pitch:

1. **Craft a Compelling Pitch Deck:**
   - o Create a professional pitch deck that outlines your podcast's statistics, audience demographics, and engagement metrics.
   - o Include information about your podcast's reach, download numbers, listener locations, and other relevant data.
2. **Showcase Your Audience:** Highlight your audience's interests, behaviors, and purchasing power to demonstrate their value to potential sponsors.
3. **Tailor to Sponsors' Objectives:** Customize your pitch deck for each potential sponsor, demonstrating how your podcast can help achieve their marketing goals.

Approaching Potential Sponsors:

1. **Identify Relevant Brands:** Research companies that align with your podcast's niche and would benefit from reaching your audience.
2. **Contact Decision Makers:** Reach out to the appropriate contacts within the potential sponsor's organization, such as marketing managers or partnership teams.
3. **Email Outreach:** Craft personalized and compelling email pitches that introduce your podcast, highlight its value, and propose a potential partnership.
4. **Networking:** Attend industry events, conferences, or webinars to connect with potential sponsors and establish relationships.

Showcasing Previous Success:

1. **Case Studies:** Share success stories of previous sponsorships or collaborations to demonstrate the positive impact on brands.
2. **Testimonials:** Gather testimonials from past sponsors or advertisers who have seen positive results from partnering with your podcast.

Offering Creative Sponsorship Opportunities:

1. **Tailored Ad Formats:** Propose creative ad formats that resonate with your audience, such as integrated segments, storytelling, or host-read ads.
2. **Customizable Packages:** Provide sponsorship packages that allow sponsors to choose the level of involvement that suits their goals and budget.

Maintaining Transparency:

1. **Disclose Partnerships:** Clearly disclose sponsorships and partnerships to your listeners to maintain transparency and trust.
2. **Integration over Intrusion:** Ensure that sponsored content integrates seamlessly with your podcast's overall tone and style.

Negotiating and Building Relationships:

1. **Negotiation Skills:** Develop negotiation skills to strike fair and mutually beneficial sponsorship deals.
2. **Long-Term Relationships:** Focus on building lasting relationships with sponsors, aiming for repeat collaborations.

Attracting sponsors and advertisers requires a combination of showcasing your podcast's value, targeted outreach, and effective communication. By positioning your podcast as a valuable platform for reaching a dedicated audience, you'll increase your chances of forming successful partnerships that benefit both your podcast and your sponsors.

Creating Value for Sponsors and Maintaining Authenticity

When working with sponsors, it's essential to provide value while maintaining the authenticity that your listeners expect from your podcast. In this chapter, we'll explore strategies to ensure that your sponsorships align with your content and resonate with your audience.

Creating Value for Sponsors:

1. **Understand Sponsor Objectives:**
   Clearly grasp your sponsor's marketing goals and desired outcomes from the partnership.

2. **Customized Campaigns:**
   Tailor sponsorship packages to address the specific needs and objectives of each sponsor.

3. **Engagement Opportunities:**
   Offer creative ways for sponsors to engage with your audience, such as interactive segments, giveaways, or contests.

4. **Data Insights:**
   Provide sponsors with relevant data and metrics that demonstrate the impact of their sponsorship.

5. **Promotional Exposure:**
   Promote sponsors across multiple channels, including podcast episodes, social media, and your website.

Maintaining Authenticity:

1. **Fit with Your Content:**
   Only partner with sponsors whose products or services align with your podcast's content and values.

2. **Host-Read Ads:**
   Opt for host-read advertisements to maintain a personal touch and integrate the ad naturally into your episode.

3. **Honest Recommendations:**
   Share personal experiences or genuine insights about the sponsor's offerings to build trust with your audience.

4. **Transparency:**
Clearly disclose sponsored content to your listeners to maintain transparency and credibility.

Integration over Intrusion:

1. **Seamless Integration:**
Integrate sponsored content in a way that flows naturally with your episode's narrative.

2. **Storytelling Approach:**
Craft sponsor messages into engaging stories that resonate with your audience and showcase the sponsor's value.

Prioritizing Audience Experience:

1. **Quality Control:**
Ensure that sponsored content meets the same quality standards as the rest of your episodes.

2. **Limit Ad Frequency:**
Avoid overwhelming listeners with excessive ads that might negatively impact their experience.

Building Long-Term Relationships:

1. **Trust and Consistency:**
Deliver on your promises to sponsors and maintain consistent quality in your content.

2. **Open Communication:**
Establish clear communication channels with sponsors to address any concerns or suggestions.

Measuring Success:

1. **Effectiveness Metrics:**
    Work with sponsors to define metrics that gauge the success of the partnership, such as click-through rates or conversions.

2. **Feedback Loop:**
    Gather feedback from sponsors after campaigns to continuously improve your collaboration approach.

By focusing on creating genuine value for your sponsors and maintaining the authenticity that your audience values, you'll ensure that sponsorships enhance your podcast rather than detract from it. Balancing the interests of both sponsors and listeners will contribute to long-term success and meaningful partnerships.

Chapter 11: Continuous Improvement and Growth

In the dynamic world of podcasting, continuous improvement is essential for maintaining relevance, engaging your audience, and fostering long-term success. This chapter explores the significance of analyzing your podcast's performance, leveraging listener feedback, and evolving your podcast's format and style over time.

Importance of Analyzing Podcast Performance:

1. **Data-Driven Insights:** Regularly monitor key metrics like download numbers, audience demographics, listener engagement, and episode popularity.
2. **Identifying Patterns:** Analyze trends in your podcast's performance to uncover which episodes resonate most with your audience.
3. **Strategic Decision-Making:** Use insights from data analysis to make informed decisions about content, promotion, and overall podcast strategy.

Using Listener Feedback to Refine Your Content:

1. **Feedback Channels:** Encourage listeners to provide feedback through surveys, social media, and direct communication.
2. **Active Listening:** Pay attention to both positive feedback and constructive criticism to gain valuable insights.
3. **Enhancing Quality:** Incorporate listener feedback to improve content quality, address concerns, and align with audience preferences.

Evolving Your Podcast Format and Style Over Time:

1. **Adapting to Change:** Stay attuned to shifts in your niche, podcasting trends, and audience interests to remain relevant.
2. **Experimentation:** Introduce new episode formats, segments, or styles to keep your podcast fresh and engaging.

3. **Gradual Evolution:** Make format and style changes gradually to ensure a seamless transition for your audience.
4. **Audience Involvement:** Engage your listeners in the evolution process by seeking their input and preferences.

Testing and Iterating:

1. **Experimentation:** Test different approaches to content, episode length, and promotional strategies to identify what resonates best.
2. **Iterative Process:** Continuously refine your podcast based on the results of experiments and feedback.

Staying Adaptable:

1. **Niche Awareness:** Stay informed about developments in your niche to anticipate shifts in audience interests.
2. **Embracing Change:** Embrace change as an opportunity for growth and a means to stay ahead of evolving trends.

Fostering a Community:

1. **Engagement Platforms:** Establish online communities or forums where listeners can connect, share ideas, and discuss episodes.
2. **Engaging with Audience:** Respond to comments, questions, and feedback to cultivate a sense of community.

Balancing Consistency and Evolution:

1. **Core Identity:** While evolving, ensure your podcast's core values and identity remain consistent.
2. **Managing Expectations:** Communicate changes transparently to your audience and guide them through the evolution process.

In Summary:

Continuous improvement is a cornerstone of podcasting success. By analyzing your podcast's performance, embracing listener feedback, and evolving your format and style, you can create a dynamic and engaging podcast that not only retains your current audience but also attracts new listeners. Remember that your audience's needs and preferences may change over time, and adapting to these changes will contribute to the longevity and growth of your podcast.

Chapter 12: Overcoming Challenges and Staying Motivated

Podcasting is a rewarding endeavor, but it also comes with its share of challenges.

This chapter explores strategies to overcome obstacles and maintain your motivation throughout your podcasting journey.

Dealing with Technical Difficulties and Setbacks:

1. **Preparation:** Equip yourself with troubleshooting skills to tackle common technical issues promptly.
2. **Backup Plans:** Have backup recording options and equipment in case of unexpected failures.
3. **Learning from Setbacks:** View setbacks as learning experiences, and use them to improve your podcasting process.
4. **Seek Help:** Reach out to online communities, forums, or technical experts when facing challenging issues.

Managing Time and Staying Consistent:

1. **Create a Schedule:** Establish a content calendar with clear episode release dates and recording sessions.
2. **Batch Recording:** Record multiple episodes in one session to save time and maintain consistency.
3. **Time Blocking:** Allocate specific time blocks for researching, recording, editing, and promoting episodes.
4. **Prioritize Tasks:** Focus on high-impact tasks, such as content creation and engagement, to maintain consistency.

Finding Inspiration and Maintaining Passion:

1. **Stay Curious:** Keep exploring new topics and ideas to fuel your creativity.
2. **Diverse Sources:** Draw inspiration from books, articles, documentaries, conversations, and personal experiences.
3. **Listener Engagement:** Interact with your audience to understand their interests and address their needs.
4. **Guest Collaborations:** Collaborate with guests who bring fresh perspectives and expertise to your podcast.
5. **Self-Care:** Take breaks, practice mindfulness, and engage in activities that recharge your creativity.

Cultivating Resilience:

1. **Mindset Shift:** Embrace challenges as opportunities for growth and development.
2. **Mental Health:** Prioritize your well-being and seek support if you're feeling overwhelmed.
3. **Celebrate Progress:** Recognize your achievements and milestones, no matter how small.

Setting Realistic Goals:

1. **SMART Goals:** Set Specific, Measurable, Achievable, Relevant, and Time-bound goals for your podcast.
2. **Gradual Growth:** Avoid setting unrealistic expectations that might lead to burnout.

Seeking Support:

1. **Network:** Connect with other podcasters to share experiences, advice, and motivation.
2. **Accountability Partners:** Find a fellow podcaster or friend to hold you accountable for your podcasting goals.

In Summary:

Overcoming challenges and staying motivated is a crucial aspect of podcasting success. Embrace setbacks as learning opportunities, manage your time effectively, and continuously seek inspiration to fuel your passion. By cultivating resilience, setting realistic goals, and seeking support from your podcasting community, you can navigate obstacles and maintain your enthusiasm for creating meaningful content.

Chapter 13: Legal and Copyright Considerations

Navigating the legal and copyright aspects of podcasting is crucial to ensure you're operating within the bounds of the law and respecting the rights of creators. This chapter delves into important legal considerations, including copyright, fair use, music licensing, and addressing potential legal issues.

Understanding Copyright and Fair Use:

1. **Copyright Basics:** Familiarize yourself with copyright laws that protect original creative works.
2. **Fair Use Doctrine:** Understand fair use, which allows limited use of copyrighted material without permission for purposes such as criticism, commentary, news reporting, teaching, and research.
3. **Attribution:** Always give credit to original creators when using their content under fair use.
4. **Public Domain:** Use content that is in the public domain, where copyright has expired or never existed.

Licensing Music and Other Audio Materials:

1. **Music Licensing:** Obtain proper licenses for using music in your podcast to avoid copyright infringement.
2. **Royalty-Free Music:** Use royalty-free or Creative Commons-licensed music that allows for legal podcast use.
3. **Stock Audio Libraries:** Explore reputable stock audio platforms to find music and sound effects for your podcast.

Addressing Potential Legal Issues in Podcasting:

1. **Defamation:** Be cautious when discussing individuals or businesses to avoid making false statements that could lead to defamation claims.

2. **Privacy Concerns:** Obtain consent before featuring private conversations, personal stories, or confidential information in your podcast.
3. **Trademark Infringement:** Avoid using trademarks, logos, or brand names without permission, as it can lead to legal disputes.
4. **Intellectual Property:** Respect the intellectual property of others and obtain permission when using copyrighted content beyond fair use.

Terms of Use and Disclaimers:

1. **Website and Podcast Disclaimers:** Include disclaimers that clarify the purpose of your podcast, any legal or financial advice, and the responsibilities of your listeners.
2. **Guest Release Forms:** Obtain signed release forms from guests granting permission to use their voices and content in your episodes.

Consulting Legal Professionals:

1. **Legal Counsel:** When in doubt, consult legal professionals who specialize in copyright, media law, and podcasting.
2. **Terms and Conditions:** Create clear terms and conditions for your podcast's website or platform to define usage, responsibilities, and potential liabilities.

Staying Educated:

1. **Stay Updated:** Regularly update your knowledge on copyright laws, fair use guidelines, and legal trends in podcasting.
2. **Resources:** Refer to authoritative resources and organizations that provide legal guidance for podcasters.

In Summary:

Understanding legal and copyright considerations is vital for maintaining the integrity of your podcast and avoiding legal issues. By respecting copyright laws, obtaining proper licenses, addressing potential legal pitfalls, and seeking legal advice when needed, you can confidently create content that respects the rights of creators and protects your podcast from legal challenges.

Chapter 14: Expanding Your Podcasting Empire

As your podcasting journey progresses, you might explore opportunities to expand your presence and impact. This chapter explores strategies for launching additional podcasts or spin-offs, creating supplementary content, and building a personal brand around your podcasts.

Launching Additional Podcasts or Spin-offs:

1. **Niche Exploration:** Identify new niches or topics that align with your expertise and interests.
2. **Segmented Audience:** Launch spin-off podcasts to cater to different segments of your audience with specialized content.
3. **Cross-Promotion:** Promote your new podcast within your existing podcast to leverage your established audience.
4. **Resource Sharing:** Utilize the knowledge and skills you've gained from your initial podcast to enhance the quality of your new shows.

Creating Supplementary Content (Blogs, Videos, etc.):

1. **Diversifying Content:** Explore different content formats like blogs, YouTube videos, or social media posts related to your podcast topics.
2. **Enhancing Engagement:** Use supplementary content to engage with your audience on multiple platforms.
3. **Repurposing:** Convert podcast episodes into blog posts or video content to reach a wider audience.

Building a Personal Brand around Your Podcasts:

1. **Authenticity:** Develop a consistent and authentic persona that resonates with your listeners and reflects your podcast's values.
2. **Thought Leadership:** Share insights, expertise, and unique perspectives in your niche to establish yourself as a thought leader.

3. **Networking:** Attend events, collaborate with influencers, and engage with your audience to build a strong personal brand.
4. **Storytelling:** Use personal stories and experiences to connect emotionally with your audience and humanize your brand.

Leveraging Multiple Platforms:

1. **Social Media:** Maintain an active presence on social media platforms to connect with your audience and share updates.
2. **Podcast Networks:** Explore opportunities to join podcast networks to expand your reach and connect with fellow podcasters.
3. **Guest Appearances:** Appear as a guest on other podcasts to introduce your brand to new audiences.

Managing Time and Resources:

1. **Prioritization:** Balance your expansion efforts with your current podcast's responsibilities to avoid burnout.
2. **Delegation:** Delegate tasks when possible, such as content creation, editing, or marketing, to effectively manage multiple projects.

Measuring Success:

1. **Metrics:** Define success criteria for your expansion efforts, such as audience growth, engagement, or revenue.
2. **Adaptation:** Regularly assess the performance of new podcasts or content formats and adjust your strategies accordingly.

In Summary:

Expanding your podcasting empire requires careful planning, creativity, and effective time management. Whether you're launching new podcasts, creating supplementary content, or building a personal brand, the key is to stay aligned with your podcast's core values, engage your audience across various platforms, and continually innovate to maintain growth and impact in the podcasting landscape.

Chapter 15

Success Stories and Lessons Learned

Learning from the experiences of successful podcasters can provide invaluable insights and inspiration for your own podcasting journey.

In this chapter, we'll delve into interviews with accomplished podcasters, analyze their journeys, and extract key takeaways that can guide you on your path to podcasting success.

1. Interview a variety of podcasters from different niches and backgrounds to gain diverse perspectives.
2. Highlight specific podcasters who have achieved significant growth, impact, or innovation.
3. Engage in detailed conversations that explore their challenges, strategies, and milestones.

1. Learn about their podcasting origins, including their motivations, initial challenges, and aspirations.
2. Understand the tactics they employed to grow their audience, engage listeners, and enhance their podcast's reach.
3. Explore how they successfully monetized their podcasts through various strategies, such as sponsorships, memberships, or products.
4. Examine how their podcast's format, style, and content have evolved over time to maintain relevance.

5. Gain insights into the challenges they faced and how they overcame obstacles to achieve success.

1. Identify recurring themes, strategies, and mindsets that contributed to their success.
2. Translate the lessons learned from their experiences into actionable steps for your own podcast.
3. Tailor the takeaways to suit your podcast's niche, goals, and audience preferences.
4. Learn from their mistakes and challenges to navigate potential pitfalls more effectively.

1. Set specific goals inspired by the success stories and strategies you've learned.
2. Incorporate the lessons into your content creation, promotion, and engagement strategies.
3. Implement new tactics and ideas based on the insights from successful podcasters.
4. Regularly assess your progress and adapt your strategies to align with your goals.

Success stories from accomplished podcasters offer a wealth of knowledge and inspiration for your own journey. By analyzing their experiences, strategies, and challenges, you can extract valuable lessons that help you navigate your podcasting path more effectively. Apply these insights to your content creation, engagement efforts, and overall podcast strategy to drive growth, engagement, and impact in the podcasting world.

As you approach the conclusion of your podcasting journey, take a moment to reflect on the impact you've made, celebrate your milestones, and consider the legacy you're leaving behind. This final chapter is a tribute to your dedication, creativity, and contribution to the podcasting community.

1. Consider how podcasting has enriched your skills, knowledge, and personal development.
2. Recall your favorite episodes, interactions with listeners, and moments of growth.
3. Reflect on the challenges you've overcome and the lessons you've gained along the way.

1. Acknowledge the number of episodes, downloads, and years of podcasting you've achieved.
2. Celebrate the positive influence you've had on your audience's lives and the community you've built.
3. Highlight the insightful conversations and connections you've formed with guests.

1. Offer advice, insights, and encouragement to aspiring podcasters who may be starting their own journeys.
2. Consider creating an episode or blog post that chronicles your podcasting experience and the evolution of your show.
3. Reflect on the values and messages you've shared, leaving behind a positive mark in the podcasting world.

1. Consider how you might continue your podcasting legacy, whether through new projects, collaborations, or contributions to the community.
2. Maintain connections with your listeners, guests, and fellow podcasters even as you transition from active podcasting.
3. Embrace the evolution of your interests and goals, and be open to new opportunities that come your way.

Your podcasting legacy is a testament to your creativity, dedication, and impact on your audience and the podcasting community. As you reflect on your journey, celebrate your achievements, and inspire future podcasters, remember that your legacy extends beyond the episodes you've created. Your influence will continue to resonate, leaving a lasting mark in the world of podcasting and beyond.

As a comprehensive resource for aspiring and established podcasters, this book includes several appendices that provide practical tools and references to enhance your podcasting journey.

Glossary of Terms

Podcasting terminology can sometimes be confusing, especially for beginners. This glossary offers definitions and explanations for commonly used terms in the podcasting world, ensuring that you have a clear understanding of industry terminology. Here are some of the terms you'll find in the glossary:

1. A digital audio or video program available for streaming or downloading over the internet.
2. A technology that enables the distribution of podcast episodes to platforms and subscribers.

3. A service where podcast episodes are stored and delivered to listeners.
4. Listening to a podcast episode directly from the internet without downloading it first.
5. Supplementary information accompanying an episode, often including a summary, links, and references.
6. The closing segment of an episode that often includes closing remarks, calls to action, and contact information.
7. A partnership between a podcast and a brand or company for advertising purposes.
8. Earning revenue from a podcast through sponsorships, memberships, donations, or other means.
9. A prompt to listeners encouraging them to engage with the podcast, visit a website, or take a specific action.
10. A written version of the spoken content in a podcast episode.
11. Strategies to improve the discoverability of your podcast in search engines and directories.
12. Data and metrics that provide insights into podcast performance, audience demographics, and engagement.

1.
   o Greeting and introduction of the episode's topic
   o Briefly explain the significance of the topic and its relevance to the audience
2.
   o Provide background information about the topic
   o Share relevant facts, statistics, or historical context
3.
   o Break down the main topic into subtopics or key points
   o Present arguments, insights, or examples related to each subtopic
   o Include anecdotes, personal experiences, or guest contributions
4.

- o Conduct an interview with a guest expert or relevant guest
- o Ask thought-provoking questions and allow the guest to share their insights

5.

- o Address questions or comments from listeners related to the episode's topic
- o Engage with the audience and encourage their participation

6.

- o Provide actionable advice, tips, or solutions related to the topic
- o Help listeners apply the information from the episode to their lives

7.

- o Encourage listeners to share their thoughts, review the podcast, or visit your website
- o Mention upcoming episodes or events related to your podcast

8.

- o Thank listeners for tuning in and engaging with the content
- o Preview the next episode or share any relevant updates

(Note: This is a fictional example for illustrative purposes. Adapt the content to match your podcast's style and topic.)

Host: Welcome to another episode of [Your Podcast Name], the show that explores [brief description of your podcast's theme or niche]. I'm your host, [Your Name], and in today's episode, we're diving into a topic that's both fascinating and relevant to our lives: the power of effective communication.

Host: Before we get into the nitty-gritty, let's set the stage by understanding why communication matters so much in our personal and professional lives. Did you know that studies have shown that strong communication skills can lead to increased job satisfaction, better relationships, and even improved mental health? It's a skill that impacts every aspect of our lives.

Host: Now, let's explore three key components of effective communication: active listening, clear articulation, and non-verbal cues. We'll delve into each of these aspects and provide real-life examples to help you understand their significance.

Host: To gain deeper insights into effective communication, I'm thrilled to welcome [Guest Name], a communication expert with over [years of experience]. [Guest Name], thank you for joining us today.

Guest: Thank you for having me. Communication is a topic I'm truly passionate about, and I'm excited to share some valuable insights with your listeners.

Host: That's fantastic. Let's start by discussing the importance of active listening in effective communication.

Guest: Active listening is the foundation of any meaningful conversation. It involves not only hearing the words but also understanding the emotions and intentions behind them.

Host: Before we move on, we received a question from one of our listeners, [Listener Name]. They're curious about how to handle disagreements in a conversation while maintaining respectful communication. [Guest Name], what advice would you offer in such situations?

Guest: That's a great question, [Listener Name]. When disagreements arise, it's essential to focus on understanding the other person's perspective before responding. Acknowledge their viewpoint, ask clarifying questions, and express your thoughts in a calm and respectful manner.

Host: Our listeners love actionable advice, so let's wrap up with some practical tips for enhancing communication skills. Remember, practice makes perfect, and small changes can lead to significant improvements.

Host: That's a wrap for today's episode. If you found this discussion valuable, please consider leaving us a review on your favorite podcast platform. Also, don't forget to visit our website at [YourWebsite.com] for additional resources and updates on upcoming episodes.

Host: Thank you for joining us on this journey to explore effective communication. Your engagement and feedback mean the world to us. In our next episode, we'll be tackling another intriguing topic that's sure to ignite your curiosity. Until then, keep communicating effectively and making meaningful connections. Take care!

(End of Sample Podcast Episode Script)

This sample script provides a structured framework for your podcast episode. As you adapt it to your own content and style, remember to infuse your unique voice and personality into each segment. Your goal is to engage your audience, provide valuable insights, and create a memorable listening experience.

Launching a new podcast involves several steps, from conceptualization to publication. This checklist serves as a guide to help you stay organized and ensure that you've covered all the essential tasks before introducing your podcast to the world. Here's an overview of the checklist:

- Determine your podcast's niche and target audience.
- Brainstorm and refine your podcast concept.
- Research potential competitors and identify your unique selling proposition (USP).

- Create a content calendar outlining episode topics and release schedule.
- Develop a sample episode outline and script for your first few episodes.
- Secure any necessary permissions for content usage, such as music or copyrighted material.

- Set up your recording space with suitable equipment and acoustics.
- Record your podcast episodes, ensuring audio quality and clarity.
- Edit and polish your episodes, removing mistakes and ensuring pacing.

- Design a captivating podcast cover art that represents your show.
- Create an engaging podcast logo and graphics for your website and social media.

- Choose a podcast hosting platform to store and distribute your episodes.
- Create an account and upload your episodes to the hosting platform.
- Generate an RSS feed that will syndicate your episodes to podcast directories.

- Set a launch date for your podcast's debut episode.
- Plan promotional materials and social media posts to build anticipation.
- Prepare a compelling podcast description and episode titles.

- Promote your podcast on social media platforms and relevant online communities.
- Submit your podcast to popular podcast directories, such as Apple Podcasts, Spotify, and Google Podcasts.
- Reach out to your network and potential collaborators for cross-promotion opportunities.

- Publish your debut episode on your chosen launch date.
- Share the news across all your promotional channels.
- Monitor feedback and engagement from listeners and subscribers.

- Regularly release new episodes according to your content calendar.
- Encourage listener engagement through comments, reviews, and social media interactions.
- Continuously improve your podcast based on feedback and performance metrics.

- Maintain a consistent release schedule to keep your audience engaged.
- Consider expanding your podcasting empire by launching additional podcasts or creating supplementary content.
- Continuously analyze podcast performance and make adjustments as needed.

Use this checklist as a roadmap to guide you through the process of launching your podcast successfully. By systematically completing each step, you'll be well-prepared to introduce your podcast to a growing audience and make a lasting impact in the podcasting world.

:

Gather a variety of catchy and intriguing episode titles from popular podcasts in your niche. Use them as inspiration to create engaging titles for your own episodes.

Example:

- From "The [Niche] Podcast":
  Episode: "Unveiling the Secrets of [Topic] with Expert [Guest Name]"

Collect podcast intros that effectively capture the audience's attention and set the tone for the episode. Use them as a reference when crafting your own engaging intros.

Example:

"Welcome to [Your Podcast Name], the show that dives deep into [Niche] topics and brings you expert insights!"

Find examples of well-structured show notes that provide a summary of the episode, links to relevant resources, and timestamps for different segments. Use these examples to create comprehensive show notes for your episodes.

Example:

- Episode Summary: In this episode, we explore [Topic] and discuss [Key Points]. Our guest [Guest Name] shares valuable insights about [Guest's Expertise].
- Resources Mentioned:
    - [Link to Book or Article]
    - [Link to Guest's Website]

Compile different examples of effective call to action phrases used in podcasts to encourage listener engagement, such as leaving reviews, subscribing, or visiting your website.

Example:

"If you enjoyed today's episode, please take a moment to leave us a review on Apple Podcasts. Your feedback helps us reach more listeners!"

Gather sample social media posts from successful podcasters to promote episodes, share insights, and engage with your audience on platforms like Instagram, Twitter, and Facebook.

Example:

" New Episode Alert! Tune in as we sit down with [Guest Name] to discuss [Topic]. Don't miss out on the valuable insights they share about [Key Takeaway]. Listen now on [Podcast Platform]."

Remember, a swipe file is meant to inspire and guide your content creation process, not to be copied verbatim. Use these examples as a starting point to develop your unique and authentic podcast content.

www.ingramcontent.com/pod-product-compliance
Lightning Source LLC
Chambersburg PA
CBHW062236290526
45794CB00006B/2304